HOW TO BUILD
A
NEW GOVERNMENT

HOW TO BUILD
A
NEW GOVERNMENT

A Guide for the Coming Revolution

Augusto Vieira

To order additional copies of this book, contact:
Xlibris Corporation
1-888-795-4274
www.Xlibris.com
Orders@Xlibris.com
109012

CONTENTS

ACKNOWLEDGMENT

A special thanks to mother. This would not be possible without your support. Mimila, you are the greatest.

Also, thanks goes to FIGU Switzerland for allowing me to use Edward Albert Meier's work.

DISCLAIMER

I hate disclaimers where the author basically abdicates all responsibility and then tells you to do as is written. So here is what I consider to be an improvement on that. I know self-responsibility is one of the pillars of a truly successful life; as such I take responsibility for my actions and expect that you do the same. You must know what you believe in and why you believe it before you act upon it. The decisions you make are your own, and you cannot blame others for your experiencing the consequences to the decisions you have made. If the outcome is not what you expected, know that we must learn from our error and not condemn them.

PREFACE

The idea of building a new government came to me while visiting my family in Rio de Janeiro, Brazil. While there it became common to see news about children, families, and innocent by standards being injured or killed during police conflicts with the so-called drug dealers. This painful and sorrowful fact did not hit home until one night I was awakened by gunshots. These were not distant gunshots. I was in bed, and on the other side of the wall from the outside, there was someone with a machine gun firing into the homes of people. I remember feeling the powerful bone-shattering vibrations of the machine gun. I remember thinking about the people who were being injured and killed that very moment—this is where building a new government became the only and obvious solution.

The Brazilian government did not care about the suffering they were causing. No government ever does. The police killed innocent people while allowing white-collar criminals to steal billions in public funds. It became obvious that government is the problem, not the solution. The next morning when I started writing this book, I began to tackle questions and issues that most people never consider. The result, what you have on your hands. This work is the fruit of my good intention, my honestly asserting what I know to be true and correct, and my contribution to humanity.

I wrote this book in 2008 but am only having it published now. Back then I was eagerly telling people what I had come up with, but people were eagerly shooting it down. It was obvious that people were not ready for what I had to offer. So I joined the ranks of those who saw the train heading straight for our civilization but could do little about it. Time passed and people changed. Now when I tell people to build a new government, they respond with curiosity, not hostility. The time is right to teach. I am not better than anyone, but I do have something to offer. We all do.

There are several reasons I wrote this book. I would like to encourage you to take responsibility for yourself; not just some aspects of your life but all of it: security, health, education, everything. You must be the master of every aspect of your life. This is the only way to maintain and ensure that you are truly free and prosperous.

I would like to show you that there is something better than democracy. Most people think that there is no alternative to democracy. This is utterly wrong. There is an alternative, and in this book, I outline the principle behind what is better.

As we see more and more riots, it becomes apparent that we have outgrown our government system. We must allow our current perception of democracy to go the way of all antiquated beliefs, let it take the same place as the sun and moon gods; let it be a thing of the past. Do not be stubborn and hold on to a false belief just because you are habituated to it. It is time to move out of our comfort zone and into greener pastures. It is our job to use our rational mind to overcome our incredulity. Let us use our creativity to imagine something we cannot see with our eyes. Take action to create something better. Be prepared to pay the price for freedom—taking full responsibility for yourself. Do not believe that our current democracy is the only and best way to do things. As you will soon find out, this could not be further from the truth.

I would like to help people do what they are already starting to do. People seem to know that governments need to change. People see the bad decisions governments make but do not know how to stop them. Especially, people do not know how to create real change without violence. In this book, I provide step by step instructions on how to go about this.

I would like to encourage you to take action. Do not assume that someone will save you. You are entirely responsible for everything that is good and bad in your life. It is only through labor that we will create the world we wish to live in. Only through work will we find the lasting peace we crave.

I wrote this book with the intent of being clear and concise. I have read many "How to . . ." books. In most I found that the author added a great deal of filler, diluting the message when the point could have been made in two sentences. I theorize that authors and teachers in general gain satisfaction at the sight of people coming to their feet for knowledge. This is often achieved by keeping people below themselves, giving a fish instead of teaching how to fish. Take no joy seeing others below you. This book is short and without fillers. It is written in basic English, using street language so that you may be empowered by what you read. The true teacher is able to see his students standing at his side, not below.

I wrote this book for those who know they do not control government. Those who know politicians never call seeking our advice. Those who know governments and politicians are looking after their own interests. Those who know asking governments and politicians to change will yield no result as most of them are very happy with the way things are going.

The need to change government will not be addressed. Yes, I am fully aware of the importance in understanding the need to change government. As a matter of fact, it is so important that this book was written for those who already know there is a need to change government. There is so much already written and so much evidence that government is utterly corrupt that if someone does not see it, then they do not wish to see it; so I will allow this group to come to their own realization in their own time.

I did not write this book for the conformists or know-it-alls. This is for those of us who have experienced the boot of the State. For those who have the boot of the State so far up their ass they are chewing on it. For those of us who know what it is like to ask the State to remove its boot from our ass and in response receive silence. These people are sick and are very content watching us wallow in our misery and ignorance.

I did not write this book to outline every single false legal, political, social, and economical doctrine that people have been taught and believe. Other specialists have written extensively on these issues, and I have little to contribute to the topic. Look for these works and educate yourself. It is your duty to seek the truth and the improvement of yourself and your society.

I did not write this book to impress you with language, rhetoric, statistics, or research. You judge a tree by its fruit, so judge this book by the results it can and will generate. I have not written this book to place myself above you as an authority on the subject. This book is for those who know that there has to be a change but do not know what that change is. If you do not see the need for a real change in the world around you, then go do something else; this book is not for you. Go volunteer, read a novel, talk to your wife, whatever! I have not written this book to tell you why change is a must; you should already know that.

Research wise, here is something that ran by my desk. According to the FBI's Uniform Crime Reporting statistics, between January 2010 and September 2010, thirty-one cops per one hundred thousand committed homicide and seventy-three committed sexual assault. Let's compare them with civilians. Only five citizens per one hundred thousand committed homicide and twenty-nine committed sexual assault. So if you had the choice to hang with cops or civilians, you are safer with civilians. I do not feel inspired to write another six-hundred-page textbook stating the obvious. If you don't know, it is mostly because you don't want to know.

I did not write this book to suggest or encourage the destruction of government. Nor is this book an attack on the wealthy. We need government, and being wealthy is good. As the title suggests, we must build a new government. Further, the goal is not to eliminate wealth and the wealthy but to help those who were left behind move forward.

I did not write this book to encourage revolution. I do not like revolutions as they are bloody. Another concern with revolution is what tends to come after: on one hand we have the freedom fighters who themselves become oppressors once they obtain the power and on the other the power-hungry and well-educated aristocracy who tell the people what they want to hear in order to obtain their trust and power, which are once again used for the advantage of the few.

It could be that this book will inspire you to build a new government that is different from what I suggest, that is fine. We must all go through our own learning curve. We are all at our own stage of development. This is natural and good. Whatever you do, think for yourself, see to it that your government is what your community wants it to be, and be prepared to learn from both your errors and also your successes.

I would greatly appreciate your feedback on any part of the book. So be sure to take a look at the book site www.new-government.com to find out news on the progress of the project and to voice your opinion.

They say there are three things you should never talk about—sex, politics, and religion. The often-cited reason being that people get defensive. I think we need to talk more about these things; I do not mean we need to lay it all out, but we need to start opening ourselves up to each other a little bit more. Do be careful to whom you confide with, but do find people you can trust. Learn to distinguish between those who truly seek the truth and those who pretend to seek the truth while holding to their own biases and preferences. This is a tremendous relationship building experience, but most importantly, from this we will start to find solutions to many problems we share.

If I were to summarize this book in a paragraph that paragraph would look like this: You are responsible for everything that is good and bad in your life. You do not have to rely on anyone to create or have that which you desire. There is no need to rely on any authority or power above yourself. You are a student and your own best teacher. We all have a piece of the puzzle, here is my share.

PART 1

Some Ground Work

Our Dilemma

We all know what the problems are. The quality of life is decreasing. Housing, energy, transportation, food, and education are becoming more and more difficult to afford. There are wars we don't agree with. Life is supposed to be getting better. We are supposed to be working less, becoming more efficient, living a better life—a life where we spend time with our family, a life dedicated to pursuing our personal growth and interests, a life where we don't have to work as much. We want a world free of wars and hunger. Yet look out the window, this is not the world we live in. Most important of all, there are no clear indicators that we are walking in this direction.

Our parents and grandparents worked very hard to build things that would make our lives better. Roads, schools, hospitals, manufacturing and research facilities all built over generations with the intent to come together and make our lives better. Once we had to walk great distances to collect water; the invention of the current water system was supposed to give easier access to better water. Do we know why things are so expensive? No. What happens when we ask to see where the money goes and where it comes from? We are denied. A population that is in the dark cannot be empowered to find solutions. This is one instance that can be applied to health, education, roads, and various other areas of our lives as an example of how people are uninformed, thus unable to find solutions.

The lives of the masses are not getting any better. We are working more and more and achieving less and less. Gone are the days when we could work, save our money, and buy a house. Given so much technology, given that we can produce more now than we did before, you would think that we ought to at least be able to afford our own home. Where did we go wrong? It is time to put our heads together and find out.

For some reason, the price of a house went up even though the value of the house stayed the same. (When I say the value, I mean that we need a house now just as much as we did thousands of years ago.) Economists and other so-called experts will come up with many complicated and impossible-to-understand explanations that essentially communicate the same message: "Your life sucks and there is nothing you can do about it." Don't believe them, there are solutions, and we must work to find them.

Despite all the issues we currently have, they amount to nothing more than symptoms of the true cause of our suffering—our lack of control. We simply do not control government, and this is the problem. Can you tell me how you can set in motion a program that benefits you? Can anyone tell me how you can pull the plug on a government program that causes you injury? I challenge you to tell me when was the last time you had any significant input into any decision your government made? Have any of your representatives ever asked you for your advice? People do not control government, and the result is bad decisions that benefit the few at the expense of the many.

The Goal

Control is the problem our current democracy is supposed to solve and yet does not. According to Webster's dictionary, democracy is a government in which the supreme power is held by the people. Under the current concept of democracy, the supreme power is viewed as the capacity to select a leader. This is not the supreme power people can have. The supreme power people can have is the power to decide. Our goal is to establish a true democracy where people make the decisions and government follows, not the other way around. This is how people can have the ultimate say on how they are governed. People can tell government what to do by essentially following the current system of voting, but instead of having the names of candidates we will have a chosen course of action such as to go to war. All you have to do is put an X beside yes or no.

The credibility of this idea really rests on the credibility of the current system. Does voting for a representative work? If yes, then we can use it to tell government what to do. If no, then you have just admitted a revolution is in order and you better start thinking of what you will set to replace the current flawed system.

Moreover, in the current system once selected the representatives discuss amongst themselves and once again vote. This is essentially the decision making process being suggested here, the only difference would be that the people will discuss amongst themselves and then vote. So as far as credibility goes we can look at the current system and see it working right before our eyes. Just turn on the television and see for yourself how the process works. To clarify how this is an improvement, let's analyze what is known as the agency problem.

Under an agency agreement, the principal (you) hires an agent (your representative) to make decisions on the agent's behalf. The problem is that the agent often makes decisions that are not in the best interest of the principal, all hidden by the agent through deception. Simply voting on who gets to decide is not enough. To solve the problem of control and establish something that is closer to what a true democracy is, we must not only vote on a representative but also on what the representative does; we must decide the course of action the representative carries out.

When the people are able to tell government what to do, government will all of a sudden be responsible for the execution of one great decision after another. You are the very evidence of this—what decisions would you make if you were in control? Will you choose to end wars, feed the hungry, and protect the environment? Or will you choose to give the super rich tax cuts, and funds for their for profit projects? People will do what is right.

Obtaining control will not be the end of all our problems but a large step to the right direction. Once in control, we will have the power to attack issues such as accountability, schooling, environment, and war; instead of having government make one bad decision after another; instead of having government steal our money, lock it into some account, and do what it wants without giving us an explanation.

Why Build a New Government?

You cannot escape government. To live without government is to live the life of a savage. When men come together, great things can be accomplished. As evidenced by the title, this book is not about the destruction of government; it is about building one that works. To this end let us quote Roosevelt:

> Jamestown Exposition, April 26, 1907
>
> As regards the first set of dangers, it behooves us to remember that men can never escape being governed. Either they must govern themselves or they must submit to being governed by others. If from lawlessness or fickleness, from folly or self-indulgence, they refuse to govern themselves, then most assuredly in the end they will have to be governed from the outside. They can prevent the need of government from without only by showing that they possess the power of government from within, a sovereign can not make excuses for his failures; a sovereign must accept the responsibility for the exercise of the power that inheres in him . . .

Given that we cannot escape government, we are faced with two alternatives: govern yourself or be governed by others. I am assuming that you have chosen to govern yourself, which leaves us with two options: reform or build anew.

Despite peaceful reform being met with tremendous resistance and yielding minimal results, people continue to go at it exactly the same way every time. Take the recent Occupy movement or even the protests to end the Iraq War. Those were peaceful attempts to inspire reform where the intended goal was never achieved making peaceful protest an ineffective method of reform. I will cover peaceful protesting later on.

Further, we cannot wait for government to change either, and here is why. Government as it is now is an institution created by some to control others. It may not have started this way, but it is this way now. The system will do what it is designed to do for those who created it. Whoever designed government did not want it changed; your desire to reform is irrelevant. This is why riot police get away with attacking people who are protesting while politicians, governments, and your representatives say and do nothing in your defense. They may give you some privileges such as voting for your next dictator, but these privileges are given and can be taken away. Your opinion does not matter. Peacefully asking them to change has not and will not yield any result. This applies to all current governments.

How does our current government really work? Well, they pass a law. Everyone must follow because the law is good. OK! Suppose a law is passed, like the ones we have today. Now what? If you break the law, they will send you a letter. You disregard that they will send someone with a suit to your house. If you disregard Suit-Boy, you will be sent a subpoena. You disregard that they will send men with guns and dogs to your house, put your door down, drag you to the curb, and make an example out of you. If you resist, they will call that resisting arrest and penalize you for that too. You see, government is all about force. This is what all those politicians do while never asking us for our input, they put control over force on their hands. Their purpose is to amass power over force so as to impose one will on all.

In the words of Harry Browne, the late American writer, "Any system that lets one person force his will on another—by confiscating resources or by compelling obedience—will inevitably break down, because everyone will want to use the coercion for his own ends. And so, sooner or later, government becomes a free-for-all to be won by those best able to deceive and manipulate." A government that uses coercion can never create harmony. This in the end will be their own undoing.

The combination of lack of interest for our concerns and force that government has, makes peaceful reform virtually impossible. When peaceful reform does not work, when your attempt to improve government by correcting their error while following their procedures yields no result, forceful reform becomes the only alternative. From this reform a new government will naturally emerge as there will be a need to streamline the flow of orders from the people to government. A stream of orders designed by the people for the people.

Building a new government is not illegal. There are no laws preventing the creation of a new government, and this should be enough to relieve any tension one feels when considering the legality of this new government. There are even laws that enable such a thing. Take the United Nations Charter for instance. In Chapter I Article 1 we find:

> The Purpose of the United Nations are:
>
> 2. To develop friendly relations among nations based on respect for the principle of equal rights and *self-determination* of peoples, and to take other appropriate measures to strengthen universal peace;

There is much to be said about "self-determination" of course. However, much of what can be said will be nothing more than a convoluted waste of time. To keep things productive, let us take the plain meaning approach. Determination: the act of coming to a decision—Webster's Dictionary. Self-determination, within the political context, becomes the act of coming to your own political decisions. It seems that the UN Charter supports us in practicing our own decision-making process. (Note: given we are talking about building a new nation I recommend reading international law, including the Law of Nations.)

This is the interpretation of this section of the Charter that benefits us. It is more than likely that courts will disagree. I will not get bogged down with much discussion about the legal side of things and I recommend that you don't either. Here is why: it does not matter what any law says, you must do what you know is right. The powers that be have a vested interest in keeping us subservient to them and one of the ways they do that is by creating convoluted laws that restrict and take our freedom. Do not waste your time going into their courts warding (word + war) with them about what you can or cannot do. Playing this legal game while others are dying of hunger, requiring people to sign this and that in order to not be a slave is utter stupidity. This is the equivalent of playing Monopoly against someone who invents the rules as you go along. If they wanted to help us, they would by educating us on how to use the law to our advantage; instead they tell us what the law is and almost always we come out losing. We all have the right to honestly assert what we know to be true, even though it may be unfounded in law. As extensive as the law is it does not cover everything. Do not rely on others to give you permission to do something you know is right.

PART 2

A Guide for the Coming Revolution

I wrote this book to help avoid a revolution. Revolutions are bloody. What tends to come after the revolution is either the freedom fighters themselves becoming oppressors, or the power hungry and well-educated aristocracy telling the people what they want to hear once again ascend to power, which is used for the advantage of the few at the expense of the many.

Revolution, according to Webster's Dictionary, means a sudden, radical, or complete change, especially the overthrow or renunciation of one ruler or government and substitution of another by the governed. This essentially describes what we are trying to accomplish. There is only one problem; can you guess what it is? Think about it for a second. Here is the answer: sudden.

Revolutions are often bloody and unsuccessful because they occur suddenly—without warning and abruptly—as they are reactive as opposed to proactive. People ignore the red flags and warning signs until things are so bad that the only alternative is violent resistance to power structures. During such a reaction, people are just trying to get rid of some problem and the mess this sudden rise generates, mixed with lack of preparation is far too intense for anyone to manage. As a result, the same power structure take over with ready-made solutions tried and tested from the previous oppressive government.

Be clear in your mind that we need a strategy—an action plan that includes a goal and clear instructions on how to achieve that goal. This is the first step away from being reactive. Formulating a strategy during the onset of a revolution will prove itself an extremely difficult task if not impossible. Without a strategy, when people rise, things unfold over the course of a very short period of time making the implementation of any solution very difficult.

There is a major global revolution on the horizon. The current unrest of the people is foaming into revolt. As the situation continues to deteriorate, a point will be reached where anything can trigger violence. The fires of revolutions and uprisings can be sparked by anything. Once a revolution gets going, it will be very difficult to re-establish an order that suits the masses. Conducting a successful revolution is tough and the key is starting early. We need to recognize and address this now before violent reactionary revolution becomes unavoidable.

In order to prevent an unsuccessful revolution and the power grab that occurs during and after it, we must act now in solving our problem of control. We must realize that unless things drastically change, there will be a global revolt that will be harmful to all. Our revolution will not revolve around fighting. We will not be a freedom from group but a freedom to group. We seek the freedom to determine what course of action our government takes. We want to establish a true and supreme democracy. We have a goal, a government we will put into place once we take the power through our calculated revolution.

In this book, we will look at both the revolution aspect of the spoken of change and what will be set in place after the revolution is over. We will conduct revolution with words and resort to force only when unavoidable. So in the spirit of preventing a power grab, let us begin by looking at the current methods used to implement change.

Protests

Does a beggar begging harder lead you to give more? You should know that government looks at us in a similar way some people look at a homeless man on the street—they do not care and have their own interests to look after.

Protesting is the equivalent of begging government to change. Politicians and their support staff are too well paid and too comfortable to have a real concern about our problems. They have no motive to change their system. Begging them to change is a waste of time.

Violence in protests is another even greater waste of time. Destroying businesses, private and public property serves no one and the cowardly protesters who stand by as others vandalize and destroy are nothing more than low-life themselves. Those things are there for the betterment of our lives.

There is a great deal written on the subject of protesting. The older works cite the effectiveness of protesting where the current writings cite the ineffectiveness of protesting. Feel free to take a look at the evidence, but I would like to brief you on something: protesting and its effectiveness is one of those paradigms people hold and protect to the bitter end, their own end that is. I do not expect such people to read this book; but if you are one of those, you can at least admit that, at best, protesting is an utterly inefficient way of creating positive change within government. You can at least recognize that there has to be a better way of creating changes in policy that does not involved walking around day after day, rain or sunshine, to gain government's attention and sympathy. Take a look at the Vietnam protests that according to its supporters ended the war, but only proudly stated when ignoring the death of some three to five million Vietnamese, the death of 80,000 American soldiers, plus countless other injuries.

The proponents of peaceful protest often ignore the various other activities other than the protest themselves. Here are some things I picked up while reading Peter Gelderloos's *How Nonviolence Protects the State*. During the Ghandi protests, activists were engaged in noncooperation, economic boycotts, and other acts of disobedience that made British imperialism unworkable. Another fact pacifists ignore is the militant leader Chandrasekhar Azad, who fought in armed struggle against the British colonizers, and revolutionaries such as Bhagat Singh, who won mass support for bombings and assassinations as part of a struggle to accomplish the "overthrow of both foreign and Indian capitalism."

There is more we can learn from his book. Black rights activists gravitated toward militant revolutionary groups such as the Black Panthers. According to a 1970 Harris poll, 66 percent of African Americans said the activities of the Black Panther Party gave them pride, and 43 percent said the party represented their own views. Then, on May 7, after continued police violence in Birmingham, three thousand black people began fighting back, pelting the police with rocks and bottles. Just two days later, Birmingham—up until then an inflexible bastion of segregation—agreed to desegregate downtown stores, and President Kennedy backed the agreement with federal guarantees.

Within days, after local white supremacists bombed a black home and a black business, thousands of black people rioted again, seizing a nine-block area, destroying police cars, injuring several cops (including the chief inspector), and burning white businesses. Within weeks, Kennedy ended several years of stalling and called for Congress to pass the Civil Rights Act. As King himself said, "The sound of the explosion in Birmingham reached all the way to Washington."

You see how much truth one book has. You do not have to read one after the other after the other to obtain actionable knowledge. This is also why I am not a big fan of appealing to those who obstinately hold to paradigms as they deep down know are no longer fitting of our necessities; how can they not know, the truth is everywhere. It could be that people have a hard time changing their thinking once the neuron connections are established; however, this does not excuse us from stretching outside of our comfort zone and adopting better strategies and uplifting beliefs.

Our friend Gelderloos continues. The Vietnam protests followed the same pattern we have already observed. Aside from the known and long protests, there were the active rebellions by black, Latino, and Native American troops. The government's plan, in response to black urban riots, of taking unemployed young black men off the streets and into the military, backfired. Fragging, sabotage, refusal to fight, rioting in the stockades, and aiding the enemy contributed significantly to the decision to pull out ground troops. The Pentagon estimated that 3 percent of officers and noncommissioned officers killed in Vietnam from 1961 to 1972 were killed by their own troops. In many instances, soldiers in a unit pooled their money to raise a bounty for the killing of an unpopular officer. "By every conceivable indicator, our army that now remains in Vietnam is in a state approaching collapse," wrote Marine Corps Colonel Robert D. Heinl in the *Armed Forces Journal* in June 1971. What is known today as a victory—the withdrawal of ground troops—can be most clearly attributed to two factors: the successful and sustained violent resistance of the Vietnamese and the militant and often lethal resistance of the U.S. ground troops themselves.

For those of you who really want to protest, here is how it ought to be done. First, be clear on how your protest is supposed to inspire change. I have not seen anyone discuss this thoroughly, and the people who are involved with protests do not seem to themselves know how protesting creates change. I guess they remember Ghandi, the Civil Rights Movement, and the Vietnam protests and think all it takes is a good march to cause change. What little positive effect protesting has probably has to do with the havoc caused in organizations and governments giving their PR departments a hard time as they gradually run out of excuses, thus inspiring reform out of fear of retribution by the people upon realizing known harm is being done.

The defendants of protest often cite the tremendous awareness protest create for the cause and use this as evidence of the success of protests. However, as we know, protests have much more than increasing awareness as a goal; they seek to change something which has not actually happened in a long time. Protests are a superb way of improving awareness but terrible at creating real measurable change. Either way, however you think protesting works, be clear about it and be prepared to explain it to others.

Second, establish a clear goal on what your protest is to accomplish and by when. Do you want to stop a bill from being passed? Will you get someone out of power? Will you put someone in charge? Be clear on what you wish to accomplish and be clear of when it has to be accomplished. Finally, march on. Be sure to compare your due date with your achievement, and don't forget the first aid kit.

The Real Uprising

Our ultimate goal is to establish a real democracy, one where the people decide the course of action, where the people decide what the best solution is. To this effect we will begin by covering a strategy to influence and alter government as it is now. It is crucial to start this right away, the best defense is a strong offence. We must stop government from destroying the environment, the lives of others and ours.

I do not recommend targeting the state/provincial or federal government. These guys are way up there and extremely well armed; we will have to face them but it is smart to delay that conflict to our advantage. Further, we do not have the knowledge to run international affairs, but this is something we will learn and master. The best strategy is to first take control of the municipal government so we can gain some experience and a better offensive position. So let's cover the game plan.

Start with the representatives running for office. Have them sign a contract agreeing to comply with the demands of the people expressed through votes. (See exhibit A, for an example) Get together in groups and demand that the candidate sign the agreement in exchange for your votes. This is not illegal in any way. It is nothing more than a private contract, completely enforceable by any court of jurisdiction. No government has the right to interfere. This contract is a real document bearing the force of law so be sure to honor your side of the agreement. In the event of a breach by the representative you will have the recourse of going to court and obtaining a court order to remove the representative from office; so instead of going to his house with the pitch forks, you can send the police to his office to place him under arrest. Just be sure to have someone from among your community ready to take over the role.

If no one will sign such a document, then you know none of the candidates are trust worthy. A better alternative would be to run yourself. Go door to door with the contract on hand educating people, signing it with them, and leaving the original with them. Once you win you can start setting up the process of receiving instructions from your constituency. Why wait for others to do for you what you can do for yourself?

One of these two strategies should work very well. If it does not, move to plan B. This strategy is more targeted at officials already in office and covers other officials we could not keep from rising to power. We will use the technology that is available to us to monitor these officials. Two things will be utilized: the internet, and any means of documenting communication with the official. It would be better if there was a known and small group of individuals responsible for each official.

On the official's Web page we will have some basic information such as personal, work and public history; address; picture; etc.; along with a record of the official's votes while in office. The meat of the site is the pending decisions, and how and why the official will vote on them. We will simply ask the official what his position is and why so we will know if we need to act to change how the official will vote. Attempted communications and final answers will be published online. Some officials will not answer; this is the very evidence that the official is fully aware that his position will not be accepted by the people hence the no response.

There are three ways to document communications: e-mail, phone, and snail-mail. E-mail is probably the cheapest and easiest. Over the phone you will have to buy some kind of digital recording device so you can upload the conversations online. Writing is probably the most expensive and complicated, but this may work well for some people as they see paper evidence as something more concrete and acceptable along with being accepted in court.

I am going to outline the complete process for communicating in writing but feel free to eliminate any step you would like. Write your letter containing the questions how and why the representative will vote, a due date for response, and have a notary notarize it. Give the notary a registered mail envelope and have him send the letter, with his own letter explaining who he is giving the official ten days to send an answer to the notary who will keep a certified true copy of the original request in his records. Once the mail is delivered, the post office will issue a certificate of delivery containing a wet-digital signature that can be saved and posted on your site. If the notary receives a reply he will inform you so you can pick it up. If the representative does not reply then the notary will issue a certificate of dishonor along with an affidavit of dishonor. Both will certify that the notary did send the letter, the content of the letter, and that the notary did not receive a reply of any kind from the official. All documents will be scanned and posted on the website as evidence to the public. Essentially, the notary is a witness to the official's no response. The notary corners the official so he will be found and have no response in the affirmative other than admitting how he will vote. *Their not responding is prima facie evidence that they know their decision will not be accepted by their constituency.*

If you think this is not fair, then you can give the official another chance by going through the process one more time while informing in writing that this is the second and final attempt to establish communication and submit an answer. Call this a final notice and opportunity to cure.

The website will document communication with the official. Keep track of every attempted communication and response if any. Aside from a website you can use blogs. Blogs follow a chronological order so follow one communication attempt at a time even those that cover more than one issue. Once a final answer is received, post it and start rallying up the troops.

Once we know where the official stands, we must tell him how we want him to vote by, over the course of a week, writing, e-mailing, or calling him en masse. When you do get in touch with him, tell him how you want him to vote.

Another option in letting him know what the majority wants is to have a petition handed to him. This is best done door to door because it will enable your community to see you so they will know who is on the other side of the computer screen. Given that this is a fairly new initiative, door to door will enable you to answer questions and address objections much like current political candidates currently do. This should also reveal who is politically active and who is not so you will know who to approach in the future for support.

There will always be those who do not support your chosen course of action—that is, how you want your representative to vote. That is fine. These people are entitled to their opinion and do familiarize yourself with the counterargument. Build a relationship with these people as well so that you may approach them in the future when you both are on the same side.

By far, the best, most efficient, and most documented method of deciding and demonstrating the community's stance on issues is by having formal votes. These votes will be done in the same fashion voting for representatives is currently carried out but instead of names of officials we will have yay or nay for the bill at hand.

It is at this point that public demonstrations and other such activities become useful. A walk is a great way to break the silence, generate awareness, connect with those who are isolated, and get some media attention, further improving awareness about the initiative and winning bodies for the cause. For this you will need educated people who can elegantly approach others and articulate what the problem is, what the solution is, and how to get involved. I do not agree with asking people for their money as this does not build relationships or a community, and recommend you be cautious of organizations that do. Instead, we should ask for their attendance in accomplishing a common goal. When you win people for your cause, their actions within their sphere of influence will have rippling effects around the world.

Now that the official knows what is expected of him, get in touch with him again and ask him the same two questions as before: how will you vote and why? If he changed, then we have succeeded. If he did not or ignores our communication, we must move to plan C. The force I speak of here is a very specific type of force. This is not the shot-gun effect we have with protesting, rushing to the streets walking aimlessly around the city or even up to random government buildings. Force must be applied to the people who are actually in charge and hold the power to decide; not their servants who are nothing more than pawns themselves.

You would think that officials would respect the principle of democracy and the demands of the majority. Unfortunately, this will probably not be the case. They do not fear being called to account for their betrayal. We cannot sue them for making a decision that is detrimental to our well-being so they feel safe. We must take matters into our own hands. Pay them a visit and give them a call at their home, office, or cottage. Just paying them a visit and being courteous is not enough. Such outcome is well documented as it was with Congressman Joe Walsh from Illinois when Occupy protesters paid him a visit at his office. He left through the backdoor and once discovered, he ignored the protesters and continued to walk out. If you doubt me, look for the video online.

In order for this type of coercive action to be effective, it must carry the clear message that it will not be peaceful forever. In order for this elegant nonviolent approach to work, it must also carry the very clear threat of future violence. To communicate this message people can display their force in one of many ways. I will mention some here: (1) form a chain around their office and do not allow them to leave or enter their work, (2) storm the office en masse with cameras and confront them but be sure to have people at the backdoor in case the official tries to leave, (3) pay them a visit at their home, or better yet (4) lynch your representative. Be creative. Whatever you do be sure that it is aggressive and intimidating. These guys only respect force as you should already know from your past documented communications.

Do not feel sorry for them, they asked for it. If it ever comes to this, you should have plenty of evidence of these officials' bigotry from the documented communication where you informed them of what the demands of the people were. That whole process now justifies force. This is the ultimate outcome of any corrupt system; it implodes upon itself as the people turn against it. If the legal, executive, or legislative branch were to provide an alternative, we would not have to resort to such actions.

According to an article written by Johann Hari in *The Independent*, a British newspaper, in 1966 Pentagon officials went to U.S. President Lyndon Johnson with a plan to end the Vietnam War: nuke the country. But Johnson is said to have pointed out the window, toward the masses of protesters saying, "I have one more problem for your computer. Will you feed into it how long it will take 500,000 angry Americans to climb the White House wall out there and lynch their President?" According to this statement, it was the president's fear of violence upon himself that prevented a tragedy.

Despite all our warnings, it is very unfortunate that these officials will probably not take us seriously. It is at this point that we must face the music and recognize that punishment is necessary and the only way. Government seems to know this—when government gave the Occupy people an eviction notice, everyone knew that if they didn't leave an army would come for them; this is why people left. The ones that stayed ended up either in jail or in a hospital. The end of the Occupy movement in Ottawa was marked by the stand of eight people against one hundred and fifty city police. "The tree of liberty must be refreshed from time to time with the blood of patriots and tyrants. It is its natural manure."—Thomas Jefferson.

Do consider what form of punishment you are willing to use upon the official. This is something you must have absolutely clarified within yourself before you set out to do anything. I recommend that you do not hold back on what you are willing to unleash upon such corrupt people; unleash upon them the worst you can think of. The possibility of taking them to jail is virtually non-existent; so I say some rough handling, injury, and death are in order. When considering such an approach, we are faced with two options: an overt operation and a covert operation.

When considering an overt operation, do know that we are clearly outmatched. This is our fault, though. We can no longer sharpen some swords and put together some shields in our defense. Those were the good old days where all that was really necessary was courage. Due to our own undoing, they now have fully automatic weapons, sound cannons, and who knows what else. Things we cannot even begin to put together. Look at what happened with the Zapatistas who rose in arms against the Mexican government; they were crushed.

Now you know why we spent countless hours in school learning how to multiply matrices and finding first and second derivatives instead of learning how to smelt iron. We are screwed. It will also be of no use building a small community isolated from the rest of society as that provides them with an X to drop bombs. Look at what happened at Waco. So if you choose this course of action, be sure you are well armed and trained. When you go to the battlefield, you give it everything you've got and don't stop until you are walking over their cold dead bodies. I am not a big fan of an overt operation and believe that when using force, we must act covertly and carefully orchestrate our efforts.

Rise in covert conflict. Guerrilla warfare is the order now. We must walk among their servants so they will not open fire on us, for fear of shooting their accountants and cooks. There are specific techniques for waging such a battle that will have to be searched by you. This will be our silent revolution of truth.

I cannot write about such a covert operation as I will probably be arrested. Further, and most importantly, speaking of such actions in public will jeopardize the success of the operation as it will lose the surprise element. Be sure to orchestrate this quietly among yourselves. Do not use the Internet to exchange ideas. Take the oath of silence and plan your work carefully. When conducting an offensive maneuver, be sure to have escape routes. When someone is captured, change your meeting locations and rendezvous points used in the event people get lost. Be creative, stealth is your weapon.

Eventually, the threat will become apparent to all corrupt officials. They will realize that they will pay a heavy price unless they conform to the demands of the masses. This is when they will do one of two things: reform or repress. I am hoping that they won't but know that we must prepare for the worst; they will likely repress. Expect local officials to be surrounded by police officers like their counterparts in the state and federal levels and be prepared to continue with your efforts even during such difficulties. Try to speak with the police officers about the noble component of our effort to win them for our cause, but be prepared to find the living quarters of these police officers to teach them a lesson as well.

And you still think violence does not work. Seems to work for politicians especially the ones you are thinking of. Isn't that the reason their security guards are fully armed and you are afraid of using violence against them in the first place? Violence does work. It works so well that it is used by them against you in oppressing you.

This is what real activism is. You start doing things yourself instead of waiting for others. The goal here isn't to convince government of anything or to influence their decision. Our goal is to permanently have the power to determine, to dictate, to choose what they will do. Governments know exactly how the masses feel about their conduct; this is why the heads of state live in mansion fortresses.

Take control of your life. Not just the easy stuff like finding work and feeding yourself. Just as you do not wait for the government to tell you where to work or what to eat, do not wait for government to tell you what is the best political action to be taken. Include in your set of responsibilities the tough job of making difficult political decisions as you will ultimately be a part of the system that will implement and experience the consequences of such decisions.

This will naturally be a difficult and long learning curve, but only because we have allowed our political decision-making muscles to atrophy. Changing our lives and implementing a new mechanism will require moving way outside of our comfort zone and stretching ourselves into new habits. This is neither something that happens on its own nor something that happens over night. It is a conscious choice. Yes, there will be errors but we will learn from them, and there will also be successes and we will learn from these as well.

It does not take a genius to see the potential outcome of such actions—civil war. The people in power are not just going to sit there and watch it erode away. I imagine people blaming me for starting the war. I take no such responsibility. The war started when politicians sold themselves cheap to corporate interest; the war started when judges allowed the guilty to walk free; the war started when police officers attacked and murdered the innocent; and most important of all, the war started when we allowed all of the above to continue unpunished. I did not start the war; I only taught people how to win it.

Aside from the threat of punishment, there are other tactics that can be used and I highly recommend as well because they are a way of taking even more responsibility for ourselves and directly affect the system that generates the physical means of oppressing the weak. The strategies I will outline here revolve around the same idea—that we are all in the end part of the system.

Get Out of the System

Yes, you are a part of the system that engages in wars and in oppression of the weak. You may not be pulling the trigger of the gun killing the innocent, but you are indirectly connected to it. Let's suppose you are an accountant. As an accountant you are doing the accounting for someone who works for a company that produces ammunition. Let's suppose you are a doctor. You are restoring to health the mechanic who services the car of someone who drives to work to build tanks. No matter how you apply this, we are all part of this system. Some are more closely connected to the actual crime, but ultimately, the system cannot work, the crime cannot be committed, without your support.

It is not that the system is inherently bad but that we are implementing it in a very selfish and bad way. We can take something like a rock and use it for shelter or to kill someone, as it is with everything. Everything can be used for good and for harm. The system is currently being used to harm and it is up to us to start making the changes for the better.

As a first step in removing yourself from the system, plant your own food. I have done it myself, it is very easy taking about one hour per day and as low as fifteen minutes per day once the soil is healthy. Here is why it works: when you buy food there is a profit that is generated by that purchase. That profit will go to the shareholders as dividends and government as taxes. Aside from the obvious environmental benefits of not adding pesticides to the soil and all such things, when you plant your own food, you are reducing the amount of money the elite has and the amount the government collects in taxes. They will have less to invest in their crap. The money you will save from paying for food can be put to good work. Be creative, donate, invest in community programs, anything.

This food idea works in other ways as well. Planting your own food enhances your freedom of choice. Some people can admit that they work for food, many cannot. Since you are reading this book, I am pretty sure you know that without work you don't eat. Now let's suppose your boss tells you to do something you do not agree with like protecting a corrupt official. Given that you work for food, your choice is either starve or obey. On the other hand, if you plant your own food, you can refuse. Food grows for free, this means that you have the right to life independent of all other humans around you. From this independence, we can start making certain decisions that benefit all.

I am using food as an example but this applies to other areas of life. Clothing, shelter, transportation, and security are all areas that we must become entirely responsible for. We must learn to produce these things ourselves so that no one will be able to coerce us into doing anything we don't want to do. This is the only way that we will eliminate the need to chase the money. This does not mean that we will eliminate money but only the need to chase it to survive. Commerce and trade are good and should not be eliminated. What needs to be eliminated is our dependence on it. Food is the simplest and easiest way to start establishing our freedom. The other things will take a while longer to learn, but it can be done.

This much control may seem difficult but it can be done. For instance, how much do you remember from you elementary, junior high, and high school years? Yeah! All of that, huh? In my case, I remember spending hours learning algebra, calculus, and a bunch of other stuff I have never used to survive or build anything useful. So instead of learning all this, why not learn how to plant your own food, how to operate the community textile capital, learn how to make your own home, and learn how to make your own transportation?

Security is very important. I know the world can be less violent and in the end perfect. However, this is not something that will come on its own. We will have to work for it. Till then we must take responsibility for our security. Responsibility for our security should not be on the hands of an armed force such as the police. Instead it should be on our hands. Police spend about one year at police academy learning how to look after your security. I think we should spend one year in high school learning exactly what they learn at police academy; this way we will be able to defend ourselves and help those in need when the moment arises.

To invest time learning such things will provide us with immense growth and development of our consciousness. These are the activities that will bring us away from the Stone Age. Even though we have wonderful things all around us, mentally we are still cavemen. We know how to press the pedal and steer an automobile but we cannot make one. Imagine what would happen if you were to get lost in the Amazon. A year later, if you are alive, you will have stone tools and some raggedy animal fur for clothing. Stone tools, the stuff cavemen are known for; we really don't know how to make anything else. Most people cannot even make copper, which is the first step away from the Stone Age. Do you see how behind we are? How little we know?

To look beyond what can be seen, to seek knowledge and truth, to do such things is to be a truly evolved human being. This is the caveman becoming a human being that lives outside of the five senses. We must take this challenge upon ourselves. After all, we know very well that school does not invest time or effort teaching us this empowering knowledge.

This is the type of knowledge that elites have mustered. Believe it or not, at the top of the pyramid are scientists. This is the type of knowledge that has made us their servants—we rely on them for food, clothing, shelter, transportation, and security. Such knowledge is available to us. Creation has not denied us such understanding. To obtain it, we must work for it just as the elites worked very hard themselves to learn how to put a ship into space or to make weapons that intimidate us. They are using the knowledge for their gain at our expense. It is our duty to use it for good.

Taking responsibility for every aspect of our lives means doing everything for ourselves. Not just the stuff we are comfortable with, everything. This will require a massive change in our lives. This change will not come over night, it will be incremental. We must make small but sustainable changes to our everyday lives and pass these changes to a new generation as a new culture.

Given that it will take time for us to work ourselves into such high levels of independence and peaceful existence, there is still much that can be done to influence the system while we are still in it. Your current work place is a great place to start. As with other things, be creative in creating pressure within your company to do what is right and to be involved with clients and other companies that exercise a concern for human dignity and the environment. Be certain that what you produce is used for good and not harm.

To name but a few other strategies, we have noncooperation, civil disobedience, work-to-rule, sabotage, malicious compliance, fragging, labor strike, lockdown, economic boycotts, and other acts of disobedience that make the system unworkable or at least increase the cost of their operation, reducing the effectiveness or efficiency of the harm being done. With these we will weaken their source of power. Do remember that some of this activity such as malicious compliance and sabotage is to be covert. You do not want to be punished for it, compromise the operation, or be kicked out of the system as we are affecting it from the inside. Hit them where it hurts.

It took decades for things to get as bad as they are, and it will take decades for things to improve. Do not get discouraged. Focus on your sphere of influence—your life, family, friends, and community. This is where real change takes place. When someone tells you that one has never done much you tell them that is the only thing that ever does.

Seizing to be involved with this system and its government and living in the same land is very possible and is the order of the day. This is largely because they cannot prove that they have title or ownership of any land. Not unless they get a document with the signature of the creator of the land signing his title to them. Do not think they own the land because they named it. You have the freedom to be a part of any organization you would like. You have the freedom to not be a part of any organization you don't like.

Then you will pass the knowledge to your posterity and this is where history stops being something we read but something we live, in the clothes we wear, on the faces of our seniors, in our language, in our architecture, and in every single part of our lives. At a glimpse we will find the lessons of the past and why things are the way they are.

Public Demonstrations

Public demonstrations are an excellent way to create awareness. So on the topic of public demonstrations, I would like to outline some points to make this effective. Resort to violence only as a means of self-defense. If the police attack you, which they probably will, defend yourself, nothing more. I am not encouraging violence only self-defense. To that end, let us look at nature. Everything that lives has a means of preserving its own life and well being. A tree has bark to shield and protect itself from foreign invaders. The grasshopper can flee danger. And the lion can eliminate that which threatens its life. The law of self-preservation is a fundamental law of life. Humans fall under the same laws that these creature honor. To do otherwise is to learn a very painful lesson. If when congregating peacefully you are attacked, do not lash out at private or public property; target the source—the police. Fall upon them with the wrath of ages and make an example of their inappropriate and unacceptable behavior.

Do not be like the current protesters who sit there being beaten and arrested by these monsters. An injured activist is as good as a couch potato. You will take up space in hospitals, and after you are arrested, you will have a host of other problems. Once you get thrown into the spinning blades of the legal system, getting out will be very difficult and expensive. It is virtually impossible to find a lawyer who is dedicated to justice and your rights as the legal industry keeps tight records on their lawyers and their conduct in court. Whatever lawyer you find will be more concerned with getting paid at least $200 an hour than with your human dignity. You do not want to get yourself in that position. If you do, I will have earned your respect for giving you this warning, as you will know that I am telling you the truth; lawyers and police are not trained to protect your rights. The legal industry is not pretty.

Prepare yourselves. When Martin Luther King was leading his walks, people were first being roughed up before participating on the walks. You can practice being roughed up, but I do not recommend it. What you need to practice is fighting off the riot police, standing your ground. Get some equipment together: motorcycle helmets, batons, shields, and anything you think will be useful. You can actually buy the same equipment that the police use. It is surprisingly cheap, look online. Get together in groups, form two opposing lines, and practice. Don't just stand there and let them ruin what you are trying to create. After all, we live in a society where equality before the law is paramount; if they can do it, then so can we. You know you are not doing any harm; you are doing something noble with your initiative. You have the right to live a good life too. Keep in mind this is only a light resistance I am suggesting, and you should know they are not just going to take it.

The Inevitable Conflict

They are not concerned with us and are too busy with their exploitive plans to maximize their profit and power, which they will never relinquish, even up to the death of the entire planet. The only way to survive is through a mass uprising against these interests to stop all wars and injustices so that we will have a chance to recover. If the powers that be truly had our interests and the planet's interests at heart, they would institute the changes themselves.

Politicians and scientists are absolutely irresponsible, from whom the power must be withdrawn and replaced by reasonable and responsible votes by the people. This can only be achieved, regrettably, by power, which will have to be exercised by the people themselves. There remains for us nothing more than the force of power alone; peaceful resistance is ineffective against a violent government. Far too long have we allowed ourselves to be fooled by those responsible, so now by peaceful means we achieve nothing.

I imagine you are familiar with the level of violence protesters all over the world are encountering from governments. This violence has been the result of peaceful protests. From the various footage collected, we know those protesters were not doing anything wrong. Those people were asserting their rights. Can you imagine what they will do if we decide to defend ourselves while asserting ourselves against specific people in power? I can. They are not just going to sit there and take it.

Things will escalate. Here is how this could happen. Police use nonlethal weapons batons, pepper spray, plastic bullets, and other such things to disperse crowds. Suppose you were to do the same when defend your rights and giving orders to your representative. What will the police do? They are going to use this as justification for even greater force against the masses—all in the name of peace of course. The next level of force to be used will be lethal force, most likely live ammunition. The people too can use live ammunition. And so the civil war begins.

Police are violent by nature. This is why they walk around with bulletproof vests, guns plus ammo. That is why they attend protests covered head to toe. They are not there to talk so don't bother. These guys are flat out sociopaths. They have no pity, mercy, or conscience. If they see you are prepared, you better know they will use that to justify more violence against you.

However, you know you are doing the right thing; not only for yourself but also for future generations. So you must and will stand against repression. People from all over the world who are sick of their government, making decisions that are not in their best interest, will have to face this. One of my greatest fears is that people will admit this to themselves only when making the necessary changes is significantly more difficult than it would be now.

Aside from direct force, governments are likely to use sabotage as a tool against our efforts. Imagine that governments realize that we are building our own homes thus ending debt. Then they will see that we are learning and winning our freedom, and when they see what we are building, they will seek to sabotage our groups and destroy our work. This is not something of the future. It is happening now. For example, in a report released by the RCMP titled "G8 and G20 Summits Integrated Security Unit RCMP After Action Report" dated 2011-06-03, the RCMP admitted to having police organizations across the country cooperate on community spying. Canada's CBC on November 22, 2011 reported that " . . . two undercover police officers—one male, one female—spent 18 months infiltrating southern Ontario community groups ahead of the June 26-27, 2010, gathering of world leaders. They were part of a much larger so-called joint intelligence group (JIG) operation that the RCMP, in its internal post-summit review, called 'likely the largest JIG ever assembled in Canada.'"[1] It is our duty to keep watch and deal with such things. These are challenges we will have to overcome. This is where a decision has to be made, comply or stand for what is right.

As we stand for our rights, the police will gradually disclose the extent of their concern for our suffering. If government rises against us as we seek freedom, we will have the choice to either comply with their demands or seek freedom. There is no half way here. Whatever road you choose, take it to the end and give it everything you got. Remember, if you choose to fight, fight with everything you have. "If an injury has to be done to a man, it should be so severe that his vengeance need not be feared."—Niccolo Machiavelli.

One day people will realize what governments have always known—force is the ultimate source of power. People will one day realize that a peaceful protest does not work against a nonpeaceful government. One day people will wake up and see the parasites sucking their hard-earned money away and realize that unless they get rid of these parasites, they too will breathe their last only before the parasites themselves perish. When the economy

---

[1]   Tim Groves, and Zach Dubinsky, "G20 case reveals 'largest ever' police spy operation: RCMP collaborated with provincial and local police to monitor activists" CBC News. Nov 22, 2011

deteriorates enough, life will become so difficult that there will be no alternative but fighting for one's life. Conflicts will start and become more intense as people realize they must take matters into their own hands. I hope this is not the day people realize what their government is and who it serves. It is in this moment of despair that the religions and even governments will be waiting in the dark for the lost to come seeking salvation. In an effort to serve the human race, I have put these ideas in writing so that there may be light in the dark. I hope that in our darkest hour people will see that there is something better—self-responsibility is the alternative.

This conflict is inevitable. Do not think you can avoid it because you cannot. It can only be delayed to our advantage. To deny this is to delay and further compound the negative consequences we are trying to avoid. In the event you must retreat, retreat; but prepare yourself to once again rise against them. Keep your rage like a smouldering fire. Let it glow undetected for as long as is needed to flare up at a given moment as an unquenchable wild fire that will consume them all. Build your government and do so without interfering with others. However, be prepared to stand your ground against those who wish to interfere. It may take some time until we can amass enough force, so lie low while you build your position.

There was a time when speaking up was all that was necessary to end the power grab, but since we maintained silence so much power has been taken that now much more than speaking up is necessary. No one will give us our freedom, we must take it back. We all were put on this earth to fulfill our potential. Had we done this before we would not be where we are now; we would not have allowed ourselves to be subjugated; we would have stood against the corrupt false leaders and their demagogues, cast them from their throne and replaced them with true leaders. Because our predecessors did not rise when it was easy, we must now rise when it is hard.

Unfortunately, cultures and peoples are stubborn. The causes of this stubbornness are varied but one stands out—fear; people look at the police and fear what could happen if they were to so much as try to truly assert themselves. This is often the case in a subconscious level, i.e. they are unaware of their fear. Regardless, this chapter serves as a compassionate hug upon those of us who have opened ourselves to face the problems of our world; and like all those who take this leap, feel pain at the sight of the life that is and could be.

Remain watchful and seek the truth at all times no matter how hard it is to face. Never cower away especially from the threats of the military class. Never cower away before authority or jurisdiction or before any enemy because we must never be subservient to anyone. Be obedient and servant only to truth and your calling in life.

People have been stripped of their power to govern themselves. The drive for freedom is taking over, a revolution is coming. Good news is there is still much loss that can be prevented. So let us start with peaceful action. We must work together to prevent the necessity of such a conflict. Contact your representative. Speak with your neighbor. Once you do the paperwork, you will know if force is necessary or not. If it is, go for it. Go for it with everything you've got.

PART 3

Attitude:
The Philosophy of Revolution

This is a delicate area that I do not consider myself to be an expert in. However, writing this book did require a great deal of change in my attitude, and a change as simple as having people vote on the actual course of action to be taken by government will also require certain social and personal changes. This part is certainly not conclusive but serves as a starting point for your own development and a way to start dealing with certain human elements that will come to the surface even more as people take responsibility. Remember that in order for there to be growth, we must first move outside of our comfort zone. This change will naturally cause some discomfort, but this is the good kind of discomfort.

The effects of changing such a component of our lives will have in our individual lives and culture is unknown at this point. All that can be said about it is pure speculation. However, this does not mean that we cannot prepare for that change. We can at least imagine what that could do to us so we can prepare ourselves to make the transition easier.

This book is about personal responsibility. In this section, I am calling to your attention the need for change not only in government but also within yourself. The change within you is what will enable the transition into a new government where the people are in charge. Remember, ethics is crucial in the creation of a better world, and ethics goes back to personal responsibility. Once in power, you must act for the good of yourself and of others.

Values

We must reassess our values. Here is an anecdote. While in university as a business student I took a financial accounting course. Typical course, dry as can be, with a typical university textbook of six hundred pages, twelve chapters. It was interesting to see that at the end of each chapter there was a bubble that took about one-fourth of the page to describe an ethical dilemma. Despite the ethical dilemma having a common-sense answer, we still discussed it in class for about ten minutes. What did this bubble say about the priorities of that course? In a book of six hundred pages, only twelve pages had anything about ethics. This was not a one-time instance. This applied to every single course I ever took, and it applies to other areas of our lives as well. In this section, I would like to cover some values that should be made a priority; values that in the order of importance have far great urgency than the bottom line and buying stuff.

We must protect the environment. The most endangered species on earth is us only because we are our worst enemy. Aside from recycling, ending the use of harsh chemicals, and all such great initiatives I would also like to call to your attention the greatest contributor to environmental degradation and the great calamity caused by overpopulation.

In the beginning, when I spoke with people about overpopulation, most would look at me as if I was from Mars. Now it is something that is discussed in university courses as part of the curriculum and am now calling this issue to your attention as it is outright imperative.

Imagine a ten-gallon fish tank. Keep that size of the tank in mind. Now add ten fishes, then add twenty, then add one hundred. Imagine them swimming. Can you see what would start to happen with the quality of water, fish waste, and the relationship between the fishes? Humans are no different. Overpopulation augments environmental pollution, makes things like food more expensive, increases the crime rate, creates wars, and makes coordinating our efforts a very difficult task. As a matter of fact, the more people come into this strategy of voting on decisions and building a new government, the more unyielding it becomes.

If we don't make the changes for the better now, the result will be major tragedies all around the world. The population needs to be at a more sustainable level. As with other things, if we don't hear it, we will feel it. To this end, I call on everyone to educate themselves on the current dangers of overpopulation and its symptoms: overfishing, destruction of rain forests, destruction of arable land, and many others. Most important of all, the solution to overpopulation is to seize births until the population level drops to a manageable level at below one billion. At a bare minimum, take upon yourself to have as few children as possible; two to replace the mom and dad or one to decrease the population. If we do, implementing this new mechanism will be easier and there will be plenty of resources left over to build whatever we wish.

Another important value that people have forgotten is the value of the human being. We have placed the profit and our own materialism above that of the dignity of others. Money is not the priority. Remember, food grows for free, you do not need money to survive. Human dignity, life, and education are among the things we must start to cherish and hold above any material belonging. We must value honor and the keeping of our word. This means that our priority ought to be to assist the weak before we get around to buying 3D TVs when our current one should do just fine for the time being; at least until we can help those in need.

It is at this point that most of you start to consider a common tenet found among those who succeed in a capitalist society—"we cannot all succeed." People have this false belief where for one to succeed, another must fail. The supporters of this tenet raise the questions of what would success be like if we all had it? They cite the lack of satisfaction in no longer being exclusive. This argument is similar to saying that you can only be happy with your sight if others are blind. You know this is not true, those who see prefer the company of others who see as well. This shared experience brings us together. We like to talk about shared experience—what we see, hear, touch, smell, taste, and *feel*.

Listen to me very carefully, if you only derive satisfaction when there is someone eking a miserable existence below you, then there is something wrong with *you*. This is not what true happiness is. The desire to be above others, to be privileged, call it whatever you would like, is one of the most important things that we must all address within ourselves. Forget the words "to be above others" and "privilege" and focus on what that thing is; yes, that desire, that feeling. That must be addressed if we are to create meaningful change.

This is one of those things I cannot help you with even though I would like to. All I can do is call it to your attention. This is something that you and only you must solve out of your own goodwill. You must look deep inside yourself and see that desire for what it is and decide if you wish to change it or not. We all know what is right and what is wrong; no one can truly decide that for you. I know many who have made this change within themselves and are perfectly capable of seeing people succeed and achieving their goals while feeling satisfied with their own accomplishments and possessions. It can be done. It would be very lonely to be the only one at anything. We like to join with others who share the same experience. It will be great to succeed and join those who have experienced the same satisfaction.

As you make this change a reality inside of you, you will also understand this: true progress only comes to lasting fruition when everyone moves forward together. True progress comes when everyone has access to education, transportation, quality cloths, healthy food, and everything else that we consider to be the best. When no one is left behind, we will experience true peace and happiness. If we are to have true and lasting progress, we must see to it that no one is left in misery. Together and only together will we truly succeed. This is a true and profound happiness and satisfaction in knowing that no one suffers in our planet.

Some have called this socialism and I do not agree with that. It is the duty of the strong to protect the weak; it is the duty of the wise to educate the simpleminded. Yes, we must provide those unable to help themselves with the basic necessities of life but this should not be imposed by government. Socialism is government imposed. We must take upon ourselves to produce such things. The difference here is that you are in charge. You are absolutely free to enter and leave at your own free will as you have the knowledge to stand on your own two feet. With your freedom you will be able to search for a community where you can be a part of in constructing that which you desire. This is not a state-run system of helping the weak. This is you planting your own food and out of your own free will planting a little extra to help the less fortunate; the ones who truly cannot fend for themselves. On the other hand, if you chose not to do so, then you have the right to not participate.

This is a love that grows in abundance and spreads through all races. When I say love, I do not refer to the desires we feel for the opposite, or sometimes similar, sex; or that "I love you man" lame kind of love. Love in this sense refers to knowing and feeling a connection with other human beings. As a comparison, the connection referred to is similar to what you feel for an object such as a car or favorite coat. If something were to come close to damaging it, you would do something about it. Similarly, when you know and feel a connection with other human beings you will seek to help them out of their misery. This isn't something that comes on its own; it is something that we must seek and create. Once created this felt and known connection will keep us united in preventing monstrosities from ever happening again. This ought to be, and is, the true and first cognition that will form the foundation for all decisions made in this new mechanism of control.

It is crucial to respect each other and oneself. All we have is each other. All we have is our home planet. An atmosphere of love is crucial so that growth and evolvement at one's own pace is possible. It is the duty of the strong to protect the week, so support community run charities that improve the lives of the needy. It is the duty of the wise to educate the simpleminded, so assist others in their education and acquiring their independence. Not with the intent of doing the work for them but to help them stand on their own two feet and take responsibility for themselves.

Another value that needs our attention is freedom. In the past century, freedom has been a value gone out the window. It seems to have been taken over by security. I suppose the idea is that in order to protect us from some imminent danger our freedom must be taken away. In reality, the opposite is true. If there is some danger headed your way, you will need even more freedom to protect yourself. The only time your freedom can be taken away isn't when there is a danger to your life but when your life is a danger to another.

We are born free. Free to do anything and everything we want. We are even free to kill others just as others are free to protect themselves from us. People must realize that our freedoms do not come from a piece of paper. Freedom comes from a higher source. The force that created us also gave us the right to choose. If you think I have to obey you or someone in government, then do provide some evidence. Prove that at birth you or government had the right to impose anything on anyone.

When speaking of such a right, consider that we are not created by any man or woman. Do you remember when you came to existence? That does not mean the beginning isn't there. We are all from an unknown source, which must be intelligent given the effect is intelligent. I refer to that primal cause as Creation. Others have called it God and Allah. It does not matter what you call it. Everything comes from somewhere. You come from your mother, your mother comes from hers, and we do not go infinitely like that into the past; it stops and starts somewhere. No man or woman created me so no one owns me. I do not have to obey or serve anyone. Politicians with their politics creating policy that the police reinforce have no right to tell me what to do. The only power others have is the power we give away. Take no man made yoke upon yourself. Take the yoke of enhancing your knowledge and understanding as this is the only thing that is worthy of you and will provide you with peace. I find laws are often in conflict with this and for me, personally, this is something I really hate about government.

Given that no one is above anyone else, we arrive at the obvious equality among all. The principle of equality is one of the building blocks of a better world. No one has the right to force you to do something you do not want to do; the only instance this does not apply is when you do harm to someone, you damage someone's property, or there is a contract where you agreed to do your part but did not. We are all equal. No one can impose their will upon you. We must stand together and support each other against the tyrants and their minions who take their advantageous position to impose their will upon the weak.

Now here is the part that will require a real change in the hearts of people. There will always be those who will try to take away your power over your property and your life. You must be responsible and accept your duty to protect what is yours and not pass that obligation to someone else, unless you are absolutely unable to do it yourself. Take responsibility, be prepared to defend yourself against an act of violence by the power hungry.

If you allow someone to harness the capacity to impose their will over your property or your life, then you will be in a vulnerable position and at risk of being subjugated. The powerful one will have a means of imposing his will upon you. It could be that the more powerful individual may not harm you, and you are free to leave your freedom to chance. However, do not interfere with the choice of others to not take that risk, as you will be interfering with their freedom, making you something to be dealt with.

To not take responsibility over the protection of your property and life is to live without self-government. Where there is no self-government there is hierarchy. If you don't do something yourself, you are asking someone else to do it for you—this is how you give your power away. If someone else does it for you, then you will not learn and will not grow from the experience. This is why we always have someone to blame and never our actions to question. Each living being is responsible for itself. We must not only learn from our successes but also from our failures. There is equal opportunity for growth in both. Without self-responsibility, the opportunity for growth is scattered in the wind to be trampled by pigs.

There is no net underneath you. No one and nothing will save you. The responsibility falls entirely on yourself for creating your safety net. Seek to free yourself and be independent and do so through your own work. You must face the fear and labor of being entirely responsible for yourself; face the fear of error. Error is not something to be condemned but examined. In a world where one always learns, it is often necessary to step into error to learn what the correct path is. This is normal, natural, and the path of growth. Eventually, you will act completely outside of government. The alternative is to be working under government doing something you should be doing without being told to do so.

We must experience and find things out for ourselves. We must move on our own path. We need to search and find. In order for information to become meaningful, you must experience it. No one can take the truth and convince you of it. No one can make you see the truth. In order for something to be perceived as truth, it must be worked for and uncovered by the discoverer, the true truth seeker. Think about what you have read and will read in this book. Ask questions. Talk to your friends about this information. This is the beginning of the true and lasting new world order.

Something else we should value is speaking up. *Speak up* and be prepared to cause disturbances in your environment. This is the way of the true hero. Silent acquiescence is immoral at its core but it is enough so that others can take advantage of a weakness that ought to be protected. Those who benefit from your silence probably argue that your silence does not give any reason to be concerned with weather you are silent or not; this is how they justify their hearts into committing atrocities. When you don't disagree you agree. We can no longer be silent. Do not cooperate with injustice by being silent. Expressed consent is not necessary. Nothing in any law says expressed consent is necessary. To stand by, in silence, and see someone doing something under your flag binds you. Your silence gives consent to rule over you. Once we speak up, our words will very likely fall on the ears of those who understand our plight. This is how we will begin finding our brothers and sisters of change.

"In my opinion, keeping silent does not mean neutrality, rather tolerance and the promotion of the political, punishment-related, religious, militaristic and terrorist atrocities. Every human who knows these things, and thereby the truth of the facts, and is silent over them, makes himself guilty of irresponsibility and of a crime against all humans who come to death or damage through political, militaristic, religious, sectarian, war-related, criminal and terrorist behaviors and actions. Neutrality means, therefore, also to be active in relation to bearing responsibility in regard to the open naming and denouncing of the existing facts and the wrong ways of behavior of all those who govern the world, as, however, also all their myrmidons and vassals who carry out their orders in ways of war, terrorism or other ways unworthy of humans. Silence is never compatible with neutrality, because this requires that the effective facts of war, terror of destruction, murder, torture, wrong punishment-orders and rape, and so forth, become openly and clearly named, and indeed in regard to all contracting parties and persons. He who is silent is not only cowardly and not neutral, rather also absolutely irresponsible."—Edward Albert Meier, July 11, 2006.

The Sixth Sense

"But Augusto how will the people know what to do? How will people know what is the right decision?" To answer these and hopefully other similar questions, let's us take a look at what I call the *sixth sense*.

In school, we are taught about the five senses: hearing, touch, smell, taste, and sight. But there is a sixth sense that is very obvious and ignored in the average curriculum—*feeling*. We have a sixth sense of feeling that is just as prominent in our lives as the other five. We feel angry, love, pain, compassion, hate, joy, to name a few. The sixth sense is often ignored with severe consequences ranging from problems with family to physical problems such as cardiac disease.

Similarly, we feel there is something wrong with government. We feel we have to rise to a better life. We feel that we must stand up for what is right. We feel what right is. This is our sixth sense flaring up. We may not know how or why we feel, but we feel and experience the awareness the sixth sense provides us. We must now face a life that goes beyond what is nice to the touch, sight, or taste, a life of the sixth sense where we do something above all because it is right. It is now that we come to realize that evil anywhere is evil everywhere. We cannot make decisions just because it benefits us; it also has to benefit the world, the future, and many other things for it to be a good decision.

PART 4

How to Build a New Government

Building a new government revolves around streamlining the process of making decisions for the government. The end result will be a government that is so different from ours that it might as well be new. This section covers what will be set in place of the old system. This section starts with the world that follows the revolution. Hopefully, we did everything correctly and there was no war. Even if there was, what follows applies to both worlds.

The ultimate act of self-responsibility is to build a new local government. You can start by speaking with your neighbors, friends, and anyone that lends you their ear. Explain to them the concepts in this section. Educate them that there is an alternative to the current democracy. Start following these instructions and eventually you will have built at new government. Your new government has the right to protect and conserve its existence. If you do not interfere with the rights of other states, then they will have no right to interfere with yours.

I have been asked to define self-government. This I will not do. If you do not know how to govern yourself, if you need the police at every corner grabbing you by the throat and telling you to stop at a red light, to not drink and drive, then you are a danger not only to yourself but also to what we are trying to accomplish. You should not be involved with this.

Forming a New Government

This new government really starts within you. So before you continue reading, try to answer the question yourself: how will your ideal government work? As you try to design your own government take a good look at your life and think of how you will relate to your neighbor. Write your answer and then continue reading to compare what I came up with and what you have.

Despite what scholars may say, there are only two kinds of government: one that obeys orders and one that gives orders. In one, you serve government; on the other, government serves you. What we have is a government that gives orders, one that we serve. The chain of command must be turned upside down. The only problem a new government can and should solve is that of control. Control must be placed on the hands of the many. This section will teach you how to create a clear chain of command where people can make sure that their government obeys them.

What I am providing you is the means of implementing whatever solution you choose. I am not here to provide the answer to each and every single one of your problems. First, this cannot be done as neither I nor anyone else have the solution to all the problems of this world. Second, there are certain answers that ought not to be give as it will interfere with your own development. Think of school. Students are given questions and when an answer is not found, does the teacher simply give the answer? The same concept applies here. This new government is designed to give you the opportunity to implement whatever solution you choose. It is your job to find the solutions. Let us begin with an overview of how this new government works.

The idea is very simple. For the sake of simplicity, let us keep the current jurisdiction boundaries of municipal, state, and federal governments. At the municipal level, we shall have local health centers, schools, and roads. Just be sure that your community has the resources and population necessary to build and maintain your infrastructures. Control will be exercised through the mechanism that runs like this.

One individual from your community will be elected to receive instructions voted upon by the people. This individual will sign a contract before the community making the promise to comply with the community's orders. I have an example of this contract at the end of this book. All orders will be read before him and given to him in writing with a specific date of completion.

The present problem of accountability is solved not only by having the representative being a member of the community and living among the people, but most importantly, by the people having physical access to the representative. This representative will be at arms' length unlike current leaders who are surrounded by armies, thus have no fear of having to be held responsible for what selfish decisions they have made. The idea here is to be certain that punishment can be brought to those who deserve it which may mean running to the representative's house with pitch forks and torches to teach a lesson, or the pink slip. You decide.

An important component of our current system is the money we pay into it through taxes. We at times hear stories of money being stolen with very little we can do to verify the validity of anyone's claim regarding the matter. To solve this problem and to provide a means of ensuring the funds are being used as intended, the bank account used for such transactions will remain open so everyone can see everything that goes in and everything that goes out of the account. The representative will be the only one authorized to make any payments from the account. The people will make the deposits. This would work much the same way your bank account and bank statement works, by posting a monthly or weekly statement in front of the representative's house or in front of the municipal office and making all deposits and withdrawals visible online.

At the municipal level we shall have the municipal courts. The decisions of such courts will be made solely by a jury comprised of members of that community. In the event of a crime involving two or more municipalities the jury will be comprised of members of all municipalities in question. If this seems too simplistic, I recommend familiarizing yourself with how your current municipal court works. Having a trial by jury is merely an improvement on what you currently have.

Second is the state level. As before, we have a representative who will sign the same contract agreeing to comply with orders and accepting responsibility for an open bank account. His residence and place of work will be accessible so he too can be open for disciplinary action. In this level we have resources that are similar to what we had at the community level but they are advanced to the point where a single community cannot afford to have such resources. Hospitals will be equipped with expensive operating rooms. Universities will have advanced research facilities. State roads will be too vast for one community to build. These resources will benefit the communities that fund them.

Finally, at the highest level we have the federal representative with the same requirements but will be concerned with international affairs. In this section we have discussed the general concept behind building a new government. We will continue by taking a look at the details of how this will unfold.

The Decision-Making Process

All three levels will have the same decision-making process. Here is how this goes: issues will be presented in a pro and con basis to all people. Hours or days later, people will vote on the chosen course of action. The order will be given to the representative in writing who will see the project to completion. In this section, we will discuss the details of this process.

We start with the identification of a problem by someone who is affected by it. The affected often know more about the problem than anyone else. Consequently, this is the individual to first call the problem to the attention of and to educate others on the subject.

The individual affected by some problem can head to the representative's office where he fills a form containing some basic information: name, address, contact info such as e-mail or telephone, statement of problem, how he is involved with the problem, causes of the problem, symptoms of the problem, suggested solutions, and a date where he will make a formal presentation educating the public on the issue. The presentation is conducted, recorded, and made available in an established location so that people wanting to know what is going on can go to this one place and know they are receiving all information available on the topic. Now that the problem has been identified, people can begin educating themselves. Questions can be submit to the deponent and answers can be posted online.

At the end of this presentation, a date will be set where other experts and affected parties can come to further educate the public and present their solutions. Experts and affected parties may also go to the representatives office and fill out the same form as the original deponent to schedule a time to present. Over time a set of suggested solutions will be compiled and available for review. These people should also be open to answer questions from the public within a public forum either online or some physical location where questions may be answered and archived. As solutions become available some will think certain facts were not presented or a possible solution was not suggested. This may be done by following the same process, going to the same venue and presenting the facts and solutions to the public. In the event there are many solutions available, multiple votes may be taken where the solutions are gradually narrowed until a final decision is reached; how this is done will vary and you should decide for yourself how your community will narrow the options.

The people, instead of the authorities, will make all decisions. For this reason, people must see to it that all requested information is provided and that they are advised by anyone whom the community regards as an expert or worth hearing. Education is crucial as it is the turning point away from the power of legislation. Education is the foundation of self-responsibility.

On a fixed date, people will vote the same way that is done when electing government officials but instead of the names of individuals we will have a list of solutions. Any voting system that you develop will work. The best that I have seen is where voters are given one slip containing the options. They vote and place the slip into a box. These slips are hand counted and stored in the event anyone wishes to double check. Speak with the organization in your jurisdiction that oversees your current election process for suggestions and recommendations.

The selected solution will be drafted and handed to the representative who must follow it to completion by the set due date, which can be set and justified by the experts when presenting their views. The drafting of the order should be done by the people. I know that every community has many talented writers. Familiarize yourself with these individuals and every so often ask one to write the order. Once an order is at hand, it will be read to the representative. The representative will then publicly accept or decline the order. The representative will receive the original while a certified true copy will be stored in the public archives at a local library along with an online scanned copy of the original.

Another option is to have the people suffering from the problem or the experts draft a solution to be voted upon by the people. This would be very similar to the current system where politicians draft a bill to be negotiated, altered, and voted. The vote would be for a complete and written solution.

As authors of the order, the people will have authority ensuring no representative will have excessive power, establishing the authority of the people over the power held by those in office. This will ensure that the people never fall to any higher authority. The representative will know his source of power and who he must answer to. There can be no mistake about this.

Discharging the order can be done through a vote where people vote either yay or nay on its completion. This, however, seems to be quite a bit of work over something everyone should already know. Therefore, the ones that were affected by the problem and brought the problem to the attention of the masses should be required to come before the public and discharge the order. Through their signature, the order is archived on the public records as completed. Now that the order is complete all receipts and records associated with it will be brought to the public records alongside the stored certified copy of the order so that others may review all associated documentation compiled by the representative in the course of its completion along with evidence of completion.

So how do we keep corruption out of discharging? To solve this you must get the facts straight. Ask yourself this question: was the problem solved? If you do not know the answer to this question then you need to gather the facts. Once you do there will be no doubts, either the discharge is legitimate or it is not.

The decision being of a municipal, state, or international nature is irrelevant because the decision-making process is the same. People will simply educate themselves and vote. The order will be given to the representative who will carry it to completion.

When dealing with state issues, this initial municipal vote will provide a solution from the community that will be presented to the rest of the state. A second and final vote will be taken to decide the best solution of all presented municipal solutions. If the vote is in regard to an international issue, the second vote of the state will be to decide on a viable solution that will be presented to other states where a third vote on the final solution is taken.

When you take this much responsibility, you will no longer have your president, police, or anyone else to blame when something goes wrong. This is not a bad thing, it is very good. We must learn from our successes and failures. We will truly learn and grow only when we experience the consequences to the decisions we make. Consequences that are solely and entirely based on the decisions we make, to the extent there is no one to point the finger but ourselves. This will provide us with the greatest opportunity for growth. With this new chain of command, the power of education will be established and the strength of legislation and tyranny abolished.

Tying Loose Ends

As with all things in life, this new government is not flawless. There are some issues, and these are addressed here.

At every single point of disseminating information, there is the possibility of deception. How do we keep people from being deceived by the experts or presenter of problems? How do we keep the experts from being bipartisan? How to keep experts from falling in corruption? How do you keep corruption out of discharging the disorder? How do we make sure the order is being followed? What are the checks and balances?

These are valid questions but questions you should have already answered. How do you keep government and current experts from deceiving you? How do you keep politicians from being bipartisan? And so on and so forth. It all really amounts to how do you know when you have the truth? If you have not answered this question already, then you better get to work because even if you choose to dismiss the suggestions in this book, you still have to answer these same questions within you current government system, whatever it may be.

There are many other finer points with this process. For example, when do people stop gathering information and decide? Once again these finer points are really up to people to solve as they are subjective and depend on cultures and customs among many other factors that are far too complex to be adapted to a single book. Whether you choose to stop collecting information when no one has anything else to say on the subject or at a specific date is entirely up to you.

Another finer point is how does one select an expert and other affected parties? One solution is to ask them for evidence they are an expert or an affected party. As with all problems there are multiple solutions. If you are looking for other alternatives you may come up with them yourself. How do you identify an expert? Doctor says he is an expert, how do you know? How do you distinguish between and superb Doctor and a mediocre one? How do you select an accountant, mechanic, and employee? Apply these same principles to your new government.

In the end I feel as if I should not answer all these questions for you. This would not be true education but indoctrination from the Augusto Political School. True education is self-education. You are your own and best teacher. You must have the desire in you to find the truth and know how to know if you have the truth or not. Once you have solved this within yourself, you will be able to educate yourself to make the correct decision when voting.

To conclude on this finer-points topic, the goal is the same regardless, educate and vote; solve whatever challenges you face in the process. After all it is in your best interest to take control of your government and have a say on how your life is run. It is impossible to solve every single little kink; every community is different and will develop different solution to their problems. If I missed something, fix it. Don't just sit there arms crossed, whining "I need this", "he didn't solved that". This is about you, your life, your empowerment. About taking control and keeping government under your thumb. This is about providing you with a means to solve your problems. Let nothing keep you from doing this. I will not struggle to logically corner you, push you against the wall to the extent you have no response but silence or agree out of fear of being seen as unreasonable. You are free not only to do as you wish but also to think as you wish. The core here is still the same, take control of government and tell them what to do. How you do that is really irrelevant.

Voting Ratios

Under the current democratic system the majority wins; majority being 50.01%. However, that 49.99% is enough to turn against the majority and cause a great deal of damage. Do you want to see what democracy looks like in the long-run? Look at Athens. Many wars have been won by minorities therefore I recommend that right from the start you seek a winning vote of 75% for any decision, with the aim of reaching unanimous consent. However, feel free to use the 51/49 ratio if it pleases you.

I further recommend that the other 25% not be neglected; this means that the initial vote is to address the concern of the majority first and the minority second. Once the issue of the 75% is solved, turn your attention to the 25% and help them. This is essential for the longevity of any civilization—the right of the individual must be respected. No one will be neglected or left behind.

A unanimous vote isn't something that will come on its own. We must work for it. To achieve a unanimous vote we must develop a high level of cohesion in our society. To improve cohesion we must become unified in our knowledge and life. To unify our knowledge make sure that everyone has access to the latest findings and the education to understand the latest research. To unify our lives set similar goals such as solve food problems first, housing second, transportation third.

To further improve cohesions we ought to also align our values: freedom first, security second, or anything else you choose. This is more difficult but can be done. Your community is unique and within this new government we have the means to choose any course of action we wish and find what suits each community, state, and nation.

Try to move forward together as a team—seek to assist those who are left behind. If you are jumping ahead, help those who are behind. To assist with this people need to open up with each other more and be prepared to have their beliefs questioned. Given we live in a society filled with sociopaths, psychopaths, and all kinds of other paths it is very difficult to open up with one another. These are problems we have allowed to grow and now flourish. We must deal with them. The time is now. You are not an island onto yourself. Together, we can achieve so much more and we must learn to coordinate our efforts with one another; passing the responsibility to someone else will not work. So learn who is who in your circle, bring the honest close to you, and ostracise the ones who need to learn to behave like decent human beings.

The Representative

Each representative will sign a contract. The contract states exactly what can be done. Anything not listed cannot be done. The people must draft this contract so as the authors of the agreement the people become the authority, just as they must become authors and authority over orders given to the representative.

To better understand the role of the representative let us turn our attention to a different concept—agency. In an agency agreement the agent agrees to make decisions on behalf of the principal. An obvious term of the agreement is that the agent will make decisions that are favorable to the principal. The current system of electing a representative is essentially an agency agreement. Now ask yourselves how often these guys make decisions that are in the best interest of the principal—us? This is the inherent problem with the agency agreement—the agent veers off his duty to the principal to satisfy his own interests. To better understand the agency problem, let's look at how the agent makes decisions that are not in the best interest of the principal.

The position of the agent is one of great power. This power is not as much based on armies but more on the superior knowledge of the agent. This knowledge/power is acquired during the process of making decisions for the principal where the agent acquires more knowledge. It is from this position of power that the agent deceives the principal into thinking a decision is of best interest when it is not.

Even within this new government the agency problem still poses a great threat. However, our new mechanism solves one big agency problem—the biggest decision the representative can make is already made for him. The biggest decision being what main course of action government takes, i.e., to go to war or not, to build a school or a hospital. The only decision the representative has to make is how to make the project happen.

Additionally, in the course of complying with orders, the representative has to make some decisions and this is where we are found once again with the agency problem. However, this problem is solved by the known location of and accessibility to the representative so the apprehension of being brought to justice will keep the representative in check.

The representative also has the ability to seek counsel from his people when faced with an ethical dilemma. Do not allow the representative to use this window to deceive. In these situations, the representative can stand in the public realm and present the ethical dilemma to the people. This can be solved the same way as before with a vote. Once the decision is made the representative will simply continue until completion.

There is always the possibility of the representative making an attempt at completing the project and returning with an "it cannot be done" response. As with everything it all really comes down to getting the facts straight. Is this the truth or not? Why yes, why not? This is where staying on top of things becomes crucial. It is your responsibility to know what is true and what is not. The new mechanism described in this book will also collapse unless you exercise the power of self-determination responsibly.

The odds of someone from *your* community, volunteering to represent, and then screwing everyone soon thereafter, while returning home at the end of the day, is pretty slim. The complete and justified lack of trust we have today will be solved with the implementation of this solution—the volunteer will be someone well known and admired by the community for having a history of community service.

The cure to our current corruption is the possibility of being held accountable for one's actions. This may seem harsh and you may think this to be a huge deterrent to anyone voluntarily becoming a representative but I would not worry about this too much and here is why. The volunteer will likely not be volunteering to steal money, especially given the way things are structured. Now if a community chooses to behave irresponsibly and make excessive demands of the representative, thus choosing to exercise their powers irresponsibly then no one will take the honorable role of representing them, and rightfully so. The new government thus collapses. The fine balance can only be achieved with hard work where the people make a conscious effort to do what is right and fair.

This brings us to another very important requirement of the representative: the requirement of being more than an obedient servant. The position is also that of an educator due to the agency component the representative embodies. As an agent the representative knows things the principal does not; thus creating the requirement to not only answer questions completely and clearly telling the whole truth; but also and most importantly creating the requirement to tell the peole what they don't know they don't know. Allow, me to explain.

There are things you know and things you don't know. Out of the things you know, there are those you know you know, and those you don't know you know. Out of those you don't know, there are those you know you don't know, and those you don't know you don't know. (If you don't get this right away, think about it long and hard as this is very important.) It is the duty of the agent/representative to educate the people on what they don't know they don't know. They have a moral obligation, as a human being, to educate the people and empower them through knowledge.

There is a tremendous need to reveal the inner workings of things—the people involved, the various interests, and how these interests are in line and in conflict with each other, especially conflicts with the interest of the people. The representative must be able to step down from the position of power by sharing the powerful knowledge with the people. This is very difficult for the representative, as a human being, to do as it requires fighting the good battle within against one's own pride and desire to be above others. Remember us talking about this in the Values section of the book, how we all have to succeed. The representative as a teacher must be willing and able within himself to see people standing at the same level in knowledge and power. It will be difficult to find someone of this character, but it can be done.

Through this people will be educated on the inner workings of projects, negotiations, and anything else that is relevant. Further, the representative must be proactive in identifying problems and communicating them to others. Naturally, it will work against the representative if others discover something that should have been communicated by the representative in the first place. People must remain on guard for such phenomena and exercise their authority responsibly.

The ultimate responsibility of the representative is to give power away and deny himself the power to decide. Here the separation between conceptualization and execution of the work is made clear. The representative will only execute orders while the people will plan what needs to be done.

The representative will also be in charge of a bank account where moneys to complete projects will be stored. This bank account will be open to all through an Internet portal or by posting the bank statement on a public location. The representative will be given authority to sign checks from this account. This will ensure that no theft occurs, that people are informed about such affairs by knowing where their money is being spent, why it is being spent, and who is spending it; and it is a great way to make sure orders are being followed.

What are the checks and balances to ensure that representatives are doing what they are actually supposed to be doing? The open bank account will address this. The checks are the checks signed from the account and the balance is the balance of the account. These should conform to the orders issued by the community.

The representative will make appropriate payments to the organizations that produce goods and services. Schools and hospitals are a bit simpler to manage as the personnel and yearly activity is fairly constant. Each school and hospital can have its own account where all can see the initial deposit and all withdrawals. It should be obvious that the representative's responsibility extends to the administrators of schools and hospitals where they too are public servants and have the same responsibility to keep all records sign and up to date and maintain all banking transactions public.

Things become a bit more complicated when we start talking about infrastructures as these are built by private companies. This is where we must conduct a cost benefit analysis and ask ourselves if the price being charged is fair. Payment will be made by the representative from the public account. I cannot stress enough the need for a cost and benefit analysis for every single investment. Look at the intangibles and tangibles, the actual cost, and the monetary benefit and savings the investment has to offer. Most important of all, look at the profit the company will gain from this transaction; that is, the amount over their cost should not be excessively high. This is seldom done and very easy to do.

Each community member upon drafting the order will also make a budget. This budget can be done using the help of experts in the field and will represent the total expected cost of the project. Each member will make his/her contribution, and the deposit will be clearly visible in the public account. Each contributor is expected to ensure that his contribution is posted correctly. Amounts to be paid can follow the example of our current incremental tax system.

Record keeping is essential. The representative must keep all records signed and accurate to be stored in a public registry where all can review the paperwork. The same applies to schools and hospitals. For example, when completing a project the representative will make payments by signing checks, he will keep a copy of that check along with the invoice to be placed on a central public location such as a library where people can walk in and see the documents and anything else related to the completion of the project.

Note to the representative: keep your own private records in the event there is a need to prove your claim.

Ideally, the representative will not charge for his service. His reward ought to be the recognition and respect of his community. I also do not see the need for this role to be a full-time position. I know you may disagree, but signing some checks and having some meetings really does not seem like that much to me. However, if you decide to give remuneration, then do not pay in excess. The representative should certainly not be paid more than the average wage for the community. Further, no other rewards in the form of special rights or special protection will be granted, the representative is equal among all.

How to Identify a Representative

We have taken a look at the representative as a role, but who is this man or woman? Answering this question will set the stage for selecting one in the first place. The representative is simply one of us. This person comes from our community—lives there, works there, is one of the people. It is someone you have access to in the event something goes wrong, the person down the street. This is the only one in charge, thus the only one that responds when things go wrong, eliminating the finger-pointing we currently experience where no one knows anything and no one is in charge.

The representative does not rise to power by one's own efforts. Instead, the representative will be someone selected to the position of authority. This not only applies to the representative but also to judges, police, military, and any other role the people so decide to be so. All candidates for a position must be carefully checked and ideally have a proven track record of selfless acts without demanding anything in return; trust is earned never given.

True leaders will distinguish themselves by not displaying any mastery over you. Instead, select the one who is wise and kindhearted from among you, the one who teaches in freedom, peace, and love. Never trust those who rely on speech, intelligence, and strategy to acquire power. Listen for those who speak from the heart, instead of rehearsed speech.

Once a competent leader is found, keep this person in power. Only depose at the first sign of corruption. Judge a tree by its fruits. Stick down and cast into the fire any that does not bear good fruit. Periodically, we will have to pull out the weeds, clear the rocks, and remove pests from our garden. Maintenance is one very basic rule of life. There is no avoiding it.

People Are Inherently Good

When I speak of building a new government and the responsibility people must take, I am often confronted with those who believe people are inherently evil and will only act selfishly when given the opportunity to do so. They say we are apes who evolved through greed and murder. We need something to contain this evil otherwise civilization would collapse. "Government", they say, "is the force that contains the evil within us;

it is government through police, law, and force that create the peace we currently experience."

This cannot be further from the truth. People are not animals. We are all well above nature and capable of extreme love, creativity, compassion, and a host of other things no wild beast knows exists. We ask questions no beast does, like how does the cell know it has to evolve? What creates laws then reinforces it? What is government if not people? So now we are people who are inherently evil being controlled by those who are inherently evil. The only thing that could come out of this is sheer evil, chaos, the destruction of all that is. Yet there is peace.

Things still work. Drivers slow down in school zones even when there is no force of law for miles. People hold the door for each other even in the absence of punishment. People are not inherently evil. It is only through freedom that the good in us is expressed; freedom such as the one provided by this new mechanism of control. Goodness is a choice, it is not imposed. Good is brought forth through education, not legislation.

I am shocked at the number of people who say, "Well, who protects you? Cops, that's who." Odds are very high that there is not one police officer where you are right now. Who will save you now if someone, one of the many inherently evil around you, sets out to hurt you? I do not know who but I know who will not—a cop—unless one will hear your call and burst in through some window to save the day. You and I both know that is not very likely. Police do not maintain the peace. You, me, and everyone else who by choosing to be considerate, patient, and loving generate and maintain whatever peace we have.

Freedom does not invoke the expression of evil but the expression of good. There are few of us who will take the opportunity to do harm and it is our duty to contain the few who do harm. This is who jails are for. In the end these are the poor souls who are mentally ill. Since we do not know how to help them, we must keep them away from us. It is human nature to also evolve and improve so we can only safely assume that one day we will be able to assist these few. Till then it is jail for them in particular the ones currently in office.

We must realize people are inherently good. What keeps our current society together isn't greed but the good in all of us. The true civilization is based on charity not greed. You promise to do your work and your employer promises to pay your wage. By keeping both of your promises the relationship flourishes. People don't just run through red lights or push others off the road. There are too many examples of how people acting out of their own good will keep things flowing smoothly. Look to your life for the myriad of examples of how people can do harm but choose not to. What we need is the opportunity to express the good in us. Laws interfere with this natural process as they impose morality on people. Anthony Burges was right, goodness is a choice. You cannot force someone to be good.

It is this wonderful light within us that will be invoked as we implement this new mechanism. It is the goodness of the representative that will keep him working hard for the people that have trusted him. It is the experts seeking to educate the masses that will ensure people are empowered. It is the people seeking knowledge to make good decisions that will ensure the prosperity of their community and of future generations.

Failure to Comply

Generally, the representative will do what is right for the community. What is likely to go wrong is an incompatibility of values between the community and the representative, or perhaps people will think that a better representative can be elected. In both cases, the community will clearly see the need for a better representative. Politely informing the representative of such a perception and finding a better fit should not be a challenge. However, for the few representatives who choose to disobey, abuse their power, and take advantage, another set of actions and attitudes must be adopted.

Compliance is a very general term that could apply to any situation. What I am driving at here is anything the community regards as inappropriate. This could be fraud, theft, corruption, you name it. We need a way to deal with this and here is how. In the event that the representative fails to comply with our demands, members will arrest the representative and set a jury comprised of members of the community to make a decision on what to do with him. The jury's decision is final and supreme. This of course is a major change from the current system of zero accountability. Here are the details.

We know where this guy lives and he does not have the benefit of private security, so putting our hands on him and calling him to justice will not be hard. This may seem ruthless to people of our time, but I encourage you to think very carefully about the peace this can provide. There is great danger of abuse of power in the absence of punishment. No representative will be exempt from unlimited liability. The possibility of being called to account for ones conduct provides a restraint upon those with power; I believe someone already said this.

No matter how good one is power will eventually corrupt. Even when one holds before one's own eyes what is considered true and good, monstrosities may still result. When one is so high the individual is no longer visible but only the masses matter. One death is a tragedy, genocide is statistic. One can commit crimes against the few in the interest of the masses. It is crucial that the people keep a close eye on their representative and see to it that his conduct is always under their thumb.

Always remember that we are all human and susceptible to being corrupted by power. It is essential to maintain watch against those who will take the opportunity of our sleep or good hearted trust to seize power. We must recognize that there are those who wish to beat us into servitude, slavery, and dependence in order to plunder us, to take from us what is properly ours. These people not only rely on the use of soldiers/police to accomplish this end but also and more importantly on deception. They use force and guile to beat us into beliefs in invented and false legal, social, political, and economical principles so that we may be bound in our thoughts and in our feelings in order for them to gain advantage over us so they can take what is ours and lead a life of pleasure and excess.

To assist in solving issues of corruption, of abuse of power, and the ultimate test of mastery over power is one's ability to give it away. The ultimate test of the representative's control over power is ones capacity to share it. This is the foundation of the representative's role in this new society of equals. His power is to serve the interest of his people and no one else's. The accomplishment of this goal will be apparent by a representative who lives and walks freely among his people day in and day out; unlike today's leaders who are surrounded by armies and hide in their fortress mansion.

You will know it is time to clean up the public offices when you are dependent on authority. We must maintain watch to guard ourselves so that we are never again beaten into servitude. We must at all times remain independent, free, and stand as equals. Trust only those who live their lives in modesty and especially display modesty in their dealings with you.

Individual vs. Majority

This book is about taking control. Once the power is within our hands we will have to be very careful with what we do with it. Once we overcome the difficulty of taking control, we will find ourselves with other problems, namely solving the problems we created through decades of negligence and apathy of our nation, foreign nations, environment, and who knows what else. Of all the difficulties to be solved then, I would like to call one in particular to your attention.

One major decision that I can see every civilization on earth coming to terms with is that of the balance between the individual and the majority. For example, let's suppose your community needs to establish a new landfill. The community or majority will naturally select a location as far away as possible. As far a location as it may be, it will likely be very close to the house of some old lady. In one scenario she will leave as it is in the best interest of the majority, on the other she will stay as it is in her best interest. When should the will of the individual be respected? When should the will of the majority be respected? When should you, as an individual, stand up for yourself? When should you align yourself with the rest of your community?

Should we seek a compromise? Following the example, should we assist this old lady in moving to a new location? What if she decides she will not move? Should we use force? When is it reasonable to impose our will on the few?

This example touches on something that we are faced with now and will be faced with as we take control of government and our lives—conflict of interest. Over time, as we come to our senses and become more unified this will not be such a great issue, but currently, it is especially given the selfish culture and sense of entitlement people have. One way provided to assist with this issue is the suggestion that the majority's interest ought to be addressed first whiles the minority second. (See Voting Rations section) But this will not suffice for all cases as it is with this scenario.

Thus, I call to you to think this through and decide how you will address this dilemma. I will not disclose my view as I do not want to spoil or influence your own internal development. Think carefully about this issue so when you take control you will know what to do.

Be advised, coercion breeds coercion. Governments that have any form of coercion grow. The growth is always gradual and virtually imperceptible. Governments are coercion powerhouses and the new government will only work if you take the coercion out of it. This requires relying on the power of education and not legislation.

Final Words

I have honestly asserted what I know to be a better way of conducting our political affairs. I consider this book the final word on revolution and I encourage you to think of your own solutions. Have the guts to face up to the turmoil of the world. Do not judge me or my life, instead look at the ideas contained in this work and address them. Judge a tree by its fruit. I am only a man but a part of the global family. This book represents my contribution and I hope it will inspire you to do your part. Establish your self-trust and inner authority. This is not easy but necessary.

Democracy as it is now does not work. Simply having others making decision for us is not enough. You want to see democracy in the long run? Look at Athens not only today but also the ruins of what was. It did not work for then and it is not working now. There is an alternative to our current democratic system and I have outlined it in this book. Like democracy, I also think humans will outgrow this new mechanism. Ultimately, we will walk closer and closer to absolute freedom and will eventually break free from many things including this new mechanism of control. This new government will serve to wean you out of the current dependence on authority assisting with the establishment of your freedom.

Know that there are those in power who will not tolerate our taking this much control over our lives. These power-hungry sociopaths have no sympathy for our suffering and will do whatever it takes to keep their power. If we really want to take full responsibility for ourselves, if we want to establish a new government where the people are in charge, then we will have to prepare ourselves to take a stance against their armies. It is our right and duty to preserve our lives and our freedoms.

It is crucial to know that revolutions are bloody. A revolution can be avoided if we address issues before they become unbearable. Do not wait for the last minute to become brave and do what is right. Now is the time to act so we can prevent the outbreak of conflicts and wars.

I hope people act on this knowledge soon. The book is a guide in that it is supposed to be short and to the point; this approach will be particularly important when the shit hits the fan, when people are scrambling all over the place for a solution. I hope this is not the time that the basic principles of this book come to be understood by the then-enlightened masses. During this dark time there will be competition. The religions along with current governments will be in that dark waiting for the weak to come to them for their ready-made solutions. I hope that before this time many will come to see that self-responsibility is the only real solution.

What I have described here is no more flawed than the people implementing it. In other words, it is not perfect. Perfection is attainable but will come only over centuries of work. People need to step up to the plate and take the power that politicians are always on the run for. Let nothing stop you from having the ultimate say in government; stop at nothing to take the power away from these institutions. Be advised that in the end, if we don't do this now and use the power for good, if we continue to be such a danger that we are not only a danger to ourselves but also to other forms of life, then the only outcome will be self-destruction so as to preserve other forms of life. Good luck!

EXHIBIT A

Contract

I, *(Representative's Name)*, here in referred to as the Representative, do promise to

1. work and live among the people who selected me and be within their arms' reach,
2. manage a public bank account and maintain all account records open for all to see,
3. keep records of account transactions and ensure all such documents and receipts are a true and honest reflection of changes to the public account,
4. comply with all orders given to me in writing,
5. never use my superior knowledge to deprive humans of the real truth,
6. never allow others to perish in misery due to false thinking or false teachings,
7. educate the people on what they don't know they don't know,
8. not only answer questions but also tell the whole truth and volunteer all other related information,
9. safeguard the truth and use the truth to destroy lies and evil, and
10. upon breach of this agreement, will be tried by a jury of twelve randomly selected members of my community where their decision is final and binding.

Any decision made by the Representative that is not expressed in writing is prohibited.

The law, venue, and jurisdiction of this Agreement is the ratified, finalized, signed, and sealed private contract freely entered into by and between both parties.

This Agreement is contractually complete and cannot be abrogated, altered, or amended, in whole or part, without the express and written consent of both parties.

I (we) have read, understand, and gratuitously agree to all the terms of this contract.

_____   _____

Representative's Printed Name   Resident's Printed Name

_____   _____

Representative's Signature   Resident's Signature
XXX Street St.   ZZZ Street St.
City, State   City, State
xxx-xxx-xxxx   xxx-xxx-xxxx

EXHIBIT B

First Letter

Month, Day, Year

Representative's Name
XXX Street St.
City, State
Zip Code

Dear (*Representative's Name*):

In an effort to further educate myself on the political affairs of my community you are herein asked to provide the following:

1. How you will vote on XXX issue;
2. Why you will vote the way you are on XXX issue;
3. Provide a response within 10 business days from the date of this letter;
4. Provide a dated, signed response under penalty of perjury with witness to signature; and
5. Send response via registered mail to the enclosed Notary Acceptor.

Request 4 & 5 are mandatory to secure the integrity of response.

Answer by any other means will be considered a non-response and will be treated as a non-response.

Be advised that *no answer* can be provided in any instance either in part or in whole, and that through *no answer* respondent is *found out, knows how and why will vote will not be accepted by constituency thus has no excuse and no affirmative response.*.

No answer will lead claimant to believe that none exists and that above facts are true and correct. Failure to file objections will constitute a waiver of those objections and will lead claimant to believe that none exists. Respondent may agree and admit to all statements and claims made by simply remaining silent.

If additional time is required to respond, a request must be received by the Notary Acceptor within 10 days of this letter.

All rights reserved and all benefit and privileges waived.

Affirmation
I, (*Your Name*), affirm that I have read and understand the above request.

In the City of (*Name of City*), (*State*)
Month, Day, Year

Your Signature
Printed Name

Notary's Verification
In the City of (*Name of City*), (*State*)
Month, Day, Year

On this day came before me the above named man, and placed his signature on this document in my presence and stated that he did so under his own free will.

Notary's Signature
Notary's Printed Name
YYY Street St.
City, State
Zip Code

EXHIBIT C

Notice of Default and Opportunity to Cure

Month, Day, Year

Representative's Name
XXX Street St.
City, State
Zip Code

Dear (*Representative's Name*):

Please be advised that the under signed made a request dated (*Date of First Letter*).

You are hereby notified that you have defaulted under said request due to failure to respond by (*Due Date*).

Party notified is a witness with first hand knowledge, expert in respective field, has failed to provide a response, and has thus admitted to presented claims.

Therefore, demand is hereby made upon you for full response to the entire request due 10 days from the date on this document.

If an entire response is not received on or before date I shall believe that the original notice is complete and correct. Your default will be accepted as agreement, settlement, and closure of this issue. This is your only and final chance to cure your default.

All rights reserved and all benefit and privileges waived.

Affirmation
I, (*Your Name*), affirm that I have read and understand the above request.

In the City of (*Name of City*), (*State*)
Month, Day, Year

Your Signature
Printed Name

Notary's Verification
In the City of (*Name of City*), (*State*)
Month, Day, Year

On this day came before me the above named man, and placed his signature on this document in my presence and stated that he did so under his own free will.

Notary's Signature
Notary's Printed Name
YYY Street St.
City, State
Zip Code

EXHIBIT D

Notary's Certificate of Non-response

Month, Day, Year

I, (*Notary's Name*), Notary Acceptor in the City of (*City Name*), witness and having first hand knowledge of the facts, affirm as true all of the following statements:

1. (*Your Name*) has hired me a Notary Public, to be a witness in these events.
2. This Notarized document is the official Certificate of Dishonor.
3. (*Your Name*) has served a requests upon (*Representative's Name & Title*) on (*Date of Service*) allowing 10 days to respond using the record number identified below:
   a. xxx xxx xxx - (Number of Registered Mail Envelope)
4. Notices were notarized, placed in registered mail envelope and sealed in front of my eyes in my presence with the address:
   a. Representative's Name
      XXX Street St.
      City, State
      Zip Code
5. Notary Acceptor, (*Notary's Name*), certifies no response of any kind was ever made by the respondent or any representative of respondent.

6. The claimant served a Notice of Default and Opportunity to Cure upon (*Representative's Name*) on (*Date of Service*) allowing 10 days to respond using the record number identified below:
   a. xxx xxx xxx - (Number of Registered Mail Envelope)
7. Notice was notarized, placed in registered mail envelope and sealed in front of my eyes in my presence with the address:
   a. *Representative's Name*
   XXX Street St.
   City, State
   Zip Code
8. Notary Acceptor, (*Notary's Name*), certifies that no response of any kind was ever made by any respondent.
9. The respondent has Dishonored both requests.

Notary's Verification
In the City of (*Name of City*), (*State*)
Month, Day, Year

I, (*Notary's Name*), under penalty of perjury affirm that I am a witness with first hand knowledge, have read the above Certificate of Non-response and do know the facts to be true, correct, complete, not misleading, and the truth and nothing but the truth.

Notary's Signature
Notary's Printed Name
YYY Street St.
City, State
Zip Code